Managing Money Made Simple

by

Wade P. Hooks

Habakkuk Publishing
Canton, MI

HABAKKUK
Publishing

www.globalempact.org/habakkuk_publishing

First published by Habakkuk Publishing: 01/05/2011

ISBN: 9780982776919

Printed in the United States of America

Unless otherwise identified, scripture references are taken from the King James Version of the Holy Bible.

This book is printed on acid-free paper.

For more information or additional copies, refer to:

Habakkuk Publishing
734.772.2079
Canton, MI. 48187
www.globalempact.org/habakkuk_publishing

DEDICATION

This book is dedicated to all those who took my advice, put it into practice, have been successful, and now have a testimony—and to all those who encouraged me to continue teaching people how easy it is to save money. My desire is that you too will be able to tell your story of success as a result of what you learn from this book.

I also dedicate this book to those who have encouraged me to put this information into book form: my wife, who put up with me through the many long and late hours of composing; my dear friend, Wendell Ayers, to whom I owe a special thanks for convincing me that there are so many people who really need this information; and to Habakkuk Publishing for their expert guidance throughout this endeavor and for making my vision become a reality.

I am also dedicating this book to my loving daughter Gwen, a first-time mother-to-be whom I love dearly. Gwen so graciously sacrificed her time to type this book. And another thanks goes to my loving son, Mark, for allowing her to assist me in completing this work.

TABLE OF CONTENTS

INTRODUCTION

Through the years, I have been able to help so many people get their finances in order. But realizing that there are so many people whom I will never personally encounter, I truly hope that this book will help to guide them.

Many people never save because they simply do not know how. Hopefully, after reading the following pages, some of you will be inspired and more knowledgeable in managing your finances.

My purpose in writing this book is to show you how easy it is to begin saving. Most of the methods you will read about here come from my personal experiences. My goal is to show you the best way to set up a budget, and how easy it is to do so. I will also show you what a simple budget will look like, including suggested prioritization. Finally, I will also show you how to get out of debt and stay out of debt.

CHAPTER 1

My Personal Testimony of Saving

I am the youngest of six children, born May 6, 1941, on what had been a plantation during slavery in rural Alabama. My father was a farmer for the first four years of my life. In those days, everything was far cheaper than it is now. You could buy two cookies for a penny and a four pack of candy for a penny.

The town where we lived was so rural that the store on wheels, or "rolling store", would come to bring the things we did not grow on the farm, such as candy. The rolling store would come only a few days of the week. My mother would give us a nickel to spend at the rolling store. At the young age of four, I recall having a strong, inherent desire to save. Everything I purchased from the store would be enough to last until the rolling store came again; I was saving for the future. The definition of "save" is to put something away for

2

the future. If a poor child growing up in rural Alabama can save, anyone can.

The remainder of this chapter will serve as a foundation that I will build upon in the following chapters. Remember, a building is no stronger that its foundation. I know some of you are wondering what this has to do with me, but you will understand it later when we get into the next chapter. I want to lay a good foundation to build the next chapter on.

Everything in this chapter is based on my childhood years from age four through eleven. When I was four years old, we relocated to Birmingham where the eight of us shared one room. One of the eight was my cousin, whom my mother had adopted. She was younger than me, so we were closer than my natural siblings, who were all much older than me. We later moved to a larger house with two rooms—a bedroom and kitchen. After a few years, things began to improve financially when everyone in the house (except my cousin and I) had income.

My mother must have known the importance of saving, because every week she would give my cousin and me a quarter to put in the piggy bank she purchased. Remember, this took place in the 1940s, when a quarter was worth much more than it is today. I was so excited to save some money. Those quarters soon turned into dollars and I thought I was rich.

Now, this next part is something that I really want you to understand because it is a great principle that I learned as a small child. This simple principle can be the impetus to your savings if you will apply it. My cousin and I had to save the quarter that mom gave us, but we could spend the quarters we received weekly from my older siblings. That was a total of four quarters, but I would never spend it all because I always felt I should save some of them. I would hide one quarter under three different houses leaving me with one to spend. I wouldn't hide them under just one house, so that in case somebody would find one, they wouldn't find all of them. Each week I would do the same, until I had quarters hidden under every house in the neighborhood. I would also hide some in my house. No one ever found any of them. When my mother baked cookies or anything that I liked, I would always put some of them away for the future. All of this stems from having that "saving" mindset.

During my childhood in the South, there were no lawns—only yards—of dirt. Rather than mowing the lawn, we swept the yard. Shooting marbles was the number one game we played. Every yard had a marble game—even the schoolyard. Our entire recess was consumed with shooting marbles; marbles were like money. If you took someone's marbles it was like robbing them of their money. Every night, I would count the marbles I had won, then hide them under the bed. When I went out the next day, I wouldn't take any of the marbles that I had won. I would borrow two, then pay them back with my winnings. In one year, I won 913. I remember this so vividly because I was superstitious and believed that 13 was an unlucky number, prompting me to throw one of the marbles away. Everything I have written about here is about saving, whether money or marbles. The key word I want you to focus on is "SAVING." Now that we have laid a good foundation for saving, let's build on it in Chapter Two.

CHAPTER 2
Can a Poor Man Save Money?

This question has been posed by the non-rich for ages, and the answer can depend on a number of things such as your income versus your debt, living "high on the hog" when you cannot afford it, not knowing how to spend money—but most important of all, having low self esteem. You must believe in yourself. The mind is a very powerful thing. It will work *for* you or *against* you and it *will* do one or the other. If you can believe in yourself, you can save, but if you doubt yourself, you cannot. Remember this always—as a man thinks in his mind, so is he. I highly recommend that you purchase another book and DVD that I have written entitled, "Is It Too Late to Become Positive After Being Negative So Long?" It will teach you how to allow your mind to work for you rather than against you. Please don't view me as an author, but as an ordinary person just like you who has put his ideas into book form. There is nothing special about me.

I have a friend who has the greatest philosophy that I have ever heard. He would often say, and I quote, "When I was born, old man CAN'T died." This man was born in rural Alabama and never finished high school, but he was debt-free at forty and built churches and schools when the city said that he couldn't. He would not let anything or anybody stand in the way of his dreams. I encourage you to develop this same philosophy. You can do anything you set your mind to if you believe and are willing to work at it.

Now that we are in a positive mindset, let's get on with how to save money. You can see from Chapter One that I grew up being very poor. My mother and father died when I was twelve years old, leaving me with nothing. But I didn't let that stop me. Keep this in mind as you read about my experiences and successes. I'm going to tell you of my success stories, but I don't want you to try to duplicate them;

rather use the concepts to create your own success stories. Too many times we hear others' stories and try to match ours with theirs, but that is a recipe for disaster.

As I mentioned in Chapter One, I have always been a saver, and this trend continued into my adult life. I asked my wife what convinced her to marry me. She told me that I was the first guy she dated who not only had a dream, but also a plan of how to fulfill it. All of us have dreams, but very few have plans of how to reach them.

This next section is not for those who have no money left over after paying their bills, but please don't get discouraged or feel left out. I have some good news for you, but I will deal with your situation in a later chapter. Many of us have been in this situation at one point. First, I want to deal with those who have more than enough money coming in, but lack the knowledge of how to best utilize it.

When I first began working for Ford Motor Company, I was 23 years old and single. Although I have always been one who saved money, I was about to learn how little I knew about the "METHOD" of saving and the secret of budgeting. I was about to have a life changing experience that would come from an unlikely source. The year was 1964, and black/white racism was very high. The two groups did not frequently interact. My first foreman was white and most people despised him. His face was unshaven, hair uncombed, clothes disheveled, and he was a very heavy smoker. Based on the opinions of others, I believed that he did not like black people. One day he pulled me aside, and what followed will forever be etched in my mind. He was nothing like what I had heard about him. He asked me my age and then he asked if I was married. After hearing my response, he put his arm around my shoulder and said, "I want to be a father to you." I almost fainted. I'll never forget his advice to me. He said, "Wade, you are a young man with your whole life ahead of you. You are going to make a lot of money on this job because we are working a lot of overtime; but never, ever base your budget on overtime because it can stop at any time. Always base your budget on forty hours because you can count on that. When you do get married never ever buy anything that you cannot pay for out of a forty-hour check. You may have to do without some things, but you don't want to put your wife in a situation where she has to work." I took his advice and it worked. My wife was working a job where her boss was giving her a very hard time, giving her poor evaluations, and treating her so poorly that she hated to go to work. She would often come home crying. During this time, I remembered what my foreman had shared with me. Because I took his advice, and kept all of our bills in check, she was able to retire. I learned so much from my foreman, but my education did not stop there. My wife and I took every class we could on financial wellness and money management. There are many ways to save and some of them are very simple, but we miss them. The best way is to participate in automatic payroll deduction if offered at your job because it's a lot easier to save money that you don't see. Put as much as you can afford away. Never try to save more than you can afford because if you do, you will withdraw it. This following method is practical and it works. I know because it has worked very well for me. Every night, empty all of your change into a large container. When I buy something that cost $1.05, I never give them the five cents, but I give them $2.00 so that I can get the change. Try this for one year and count the change, you will be surprised! A friend of mine has a container with a lid that counts the change as you drop it in. I was with him recently and in less than a year, his container is about two-thirds full and contains $207! Another good way to save is to put one dollar into a shoebox every day for one year. Following this method, in one year you would have saved $365; $2 per day

= $730; $3 = $1,095; $4 = $1,460; $5 = $1,825 – you get the picture. Another money-saving technique is to save every quarter you get, or dime, or nickel for a year. Again, you'll be surprised!! Begin in the first week of December to save for Christmas the following year. In one year, the results will be: saving five dollars per week = $260; $10 per week = 520; $25 = $1300. The same method will work to save for vacation.

When I began working, my goal was to save $100 in every denomination from pennies to $100 bills, and I did it. When two-dollar bills were still in circulation, I would save every one that I could find. The ushers in church would collect them from the offering plate, bring them to me, and I would give them the equivalent in other bills. My goal was to save $100 in two-dollar bills, but one day when I counted, they totaled $400! I would also save new quarters and old quarters along with all the other coins. I would wrap them and place them in shoeboxes. When I checked to see how much money I had, the total shocked me. There was $4000 in coins! Hopefully, through my showing you some simple saving methods, you will use some or all of these ideas to get started with your own saving.

CHAPTER 3
Budgeting—How Does It Work?

First, let's clear up the myth that a budget is a bad thing and is only for large corporations and the government. Just the opposite is true. A budget is actually better for the average person. Budgeting simply means adjusting expenses to income or estimating the cost of operating. In other words, budgeting begins when you put your bills in order to see if your income is equal to or greater than your bills. A budget will only work as it is should if your income is greater than your expenses. If this is not true in your case, this chapter will not help you until you eliminate some of your debt. (I will show you how to do that in a later chapter.)

How do I know whether I qualify for this chapter or need to wait for the one on getting out of debt? Well, it's very simple. Just take a blank sheet of paper and draw a straight line from top to bottom through the center of the paper. On the top right side, write the amount of your total bring-home pay (do not include overtime). This figure must be the money that you consistently bring home per month. Then, on the left side, list all of your monthly expenses. It is crucial that you include everything that you consistently pay each month, including church tithes and offerings, vacation expenses, Christmas spending, groceries, medicines and personal items, entertainment, mortgage/rent, utilities, credit cards, car payments, etc. And don't forget to include the costs associated with going to work: gas, coffee, lunch, etc. When all of this is complete, add everything up and take a look. Hopefully, the income column exceeds your expenses column. If so, you are ready for your budget.

Your budget must be prioritized, beginning at the top. It is very common for people to pay everyone except themselves. You must look at yourself as a "bill" or "expense." How do we know how much to pay ourselves? Well, I'm going to give you the recommended amount. You may not be able to do this, but it is the rule-of-thumb so-to-speak. This is just a guideline, and you have to use your own figures to fit your budget. If you tithe to your church, the first money goes to the church. Then, you should also pay yourself a tenth of your income. The only bill that should come before you is God. Then third, you should save for Christmas. Later, I will give you some figures to choose from. Fourth, you should save for vacation. The remaining money can be prioritized in whatever order you choose—emergency, mortgage, car, utilities, recreation, entertainment, insurance, etc.

On the next page, I will set up a mock budget so you can see what your budget might be. The next thing you need to do is take your total expense amount and divide that number by four. This will tell you how much money you need to put into the checking on a weekly basis. You are okay as long as your expenses do not exceed your income; and even if they are the same, you are still okay because your expenses include everything you need, including spending money.

Now here is the good part. By putting this money into an account weekly, you will have a surplus at the end of year because you are basing your budget on a four-week month. About four months per year have five weeks. Remember you are putting the same amount in the bank for 52 weeks. This is one of the wonderful things about a budget. If you do have some money left over because your income exceeds expenses, this is called discretionary income. So many times we will pocket that money; but why do that when you already have your spending money? I recommend that you put this into your emergency fund. For an example, let's say your discretionary money is $100 and you put it into your emergency fund for one year without having an emergency. You now have $1200 to use just in case you have an emergency. Let's say you make it through another year without an emergency; now you have $2400! You will be tempted to withdraw some of it, but don't. Let it continue to grow so that when you do have an emergency, you won't have to borrow money or use your credit card. Your budget will look like this:

Expenses = $3900	Monthly Income = $5200
Tithe..............................$500	
Personal $500	
Christmas.......................$100	
($1200 per year)	
Vacation.........................$400	
($4800 per year)	
Emergency.....................$100	
Mortgage......................$1000	
Car................................$350	
Utilities..........................$350	
Food..............................$400	
Recreation.....................$100	
Car Insurance................$100	
Put into checking weekly...........$975	
Discretionary income..............$1300	

These figures are based on months that have four weeks. Keep in mind that there are at least four months of the year that have five Fridays. You are putting $975 per week into your checking account, which means you will gain four extra weeks per year. At $975 per week, you will gain an extra $3900 per year. How do you like those apples? This is yet another plus of having a budget. You may have noticed that I based your utilities, including your gas, on winter months. Your gas bill will decrease in the summer months, but be sure to continue to deposit the same amount into your checking account as you did during the winter months. At the beginning of the next winter you will have a surplus.

Can you see why a budget is such a beneficial thing? The dollar amount in this budget may or may not be realistic for you, but it can be a guideline to follow with your actual numbers. The key to any budget is consistency, and you must not miss even one week because it will throw the whole budget off. If you get paid bi-weekly or monthly, it will work the same. If you get paid bi-weekly just double the amount. The bi-weekly deposit would be double the one week amount which would be $1950, and once per month will be

$3900. Get it? Now sit down together and make your own

budget based on your own monthly income.

CHAPTER 4
How to Know If I Can Afford It

It is a very simple formula that was taught to me by my first foreman at Ford Motor Company. If you do not apply it when purchasing a big-ticket item, you could be getting in over your head. This doesn't necessarily mean that you cannot make the payments, but it could seriously affect your ability to meet your obligations. Here is the formula: anytime any one monthly bill is more than one week's paycheck, this is an indication that is it not affordable. For example: if your monthly payment is $501 and your weekly check is $500, your payment is too high. Anytime it will take any portion of a second check to pay a monthly bill, don't buy it! Far too many people fall into this trap. They either don't know the formula or choose to ignore it and wonder why they are having such a hard time keeping up with their obligations. A rule of thumb is "it's not how much we have coming in, but how we spend it." One once said, "My people perish for a lack of knowledge." There is another saying that goes like

22

this: "It is a fool who doesn't know but doesn't know he doesn't know and won't admit he doesn't know that he doesn't know, but won't seek help—but it is a wise man that doesn't know and will admit he doesn't and will seek knowledge." The only way you can get the help that you need to start a budget is to admit that you need help. My wife and I have used this formula for 45 years and it has worked wonders. It really made a difference in the way we pay our bills. My wife knew about and used this formula before we were married, and I am so thankful that I not only heard about it, but embraced it.

I will discuss this formula in the following chapters. I will also discuss the danger of credit cards, what kind of insurance to buy, who to cover, how much to purchase, why we need insurance, how to get out of debt, and how to stay out of debt. You will gain some very crucial information that could save you a lot of time and money. Someone said that "we would do better if we knew better." Now that you know better, are you going to do better?

There are many people who become ill and go to the doctor to get help. After an examination, the doctor may smile and say to himself, "This is an easy fix." After explaining his diagnosis to you, he tells you your illness can easily be cured with a prescription. He assures you that if you take all of the medication your ailment will disappear. The key word is "ALL" because so many people will take their prescription only until they begin to feel better. Then soon after they stop, the ailment returns and they must revisit the doctor.

It is much the same with this book. I have identified your ailment, written a prescription (this book), but unless you take all of it, your ailment will return. The choice is yours; you can take the entire prescription and be healed or take part of it or none of it and remain sickly. If you leave one part out of your budget, it will be of no effect; or if you miss one week, you have thrown a monkey wrench into a well-oiled machine. You must believe in the concept of your budget; if you don't, you won't be dedicated to it.

For those who have been on the bottom of the totem pole so long until you believe that is where you belong, you must destroy that old mindset and see yourself on the top. The mind is a very powerful thing and as a man thinks, so is he. In other words, you are who or what you think you are. Think big and you'll be big. Let nobody or nothing stop you from reaching your goal, but use every stumbling block as a stepping stone.

There is a story of a man who owned a goat that he hated. This intense hatred led him to a decision to kill the goat by burying him alive. He ordered a truckload of dirt until he had enough to fill a well. He threw the little goat into the well and began to shovel dirt down to top of him with the intent of burying him alive. After he had filled the entire well with dirt, there stood the little goat on top of the dirt. You see, every time the man would throw a shovel of dirt on top of the little goat, he would shake it off and stay on top of it. He had a choice of standing there buried or simply using the dirt as a stepping stone.

You too have a choice. Which will you choose?

CHAPTER 5
Is It Okay to Own a Credit Card?

The answer to this question is "yes" and "no." It all depends on the mentality of the person, his ability to pay, his willingness to pay when payments are due, his knowledge and understanding of interest, and most of all his credibility. If he has all of these things under control the answer is "yes"; but if any one of them is missing, the answer would be "no." It is much like asking if it is okay to own a gun, a knife, or a car. The answer would depend on the mentality and/or the stability of the person who owns them. None of these things within themselves are dangerous, but in the hands of the wrong person, they all could be disastrous.

The same is true with a credit card. If a person is in control, responsible, and a good money manager, a credit card can be a wonderful tool to have. There are some things for which you must have credit cards. Car rentals and cruise ships are two examples. I have owned credit cards, and have used them so sparingly that I have received letters from the credit card company threatening to cancel it if I did not increase my use. The few times I do use credit cards, I make sure that I have the money to pay the bill in full when it arrives. My wife has a credit card that pays her for using it. She only uses it to get the bonus, and she always pays it off when the bill comes. A credit card is only good in the hands of a disciplined and responsible person. The use of a credit card by a non-disciplined or irresponsible person is a recipe for disaster. One of the worst things you can do is use a credit card as a paycheck.

Far too many people get themselves into deep trouble for several reasons, but the most common reason is they don't understand interest or minimum payment. These are the two areas where the credit card companies make their money. Let me see if I can break them down so that you can understand them. The rule of thumb is that anything greater than seven percent interest is too high. Let me first of all try to make clear what "percentage" means. It works much like a fraction in terms of being a part of a whole such as 1 of 100. I believe I can better explain it by using the number 100. It is really simple when you understand it. One percent of $100 is $1, 2% is $3, and 3% is $3, and so on.

Now let's see how this relates to credit card interest. Some credit cards have interest rates of 21% or more, which is outrageous. So when your interest rate is 21%, it means that they are going to charge you $21 for every $100 you owe them. You may be thinking that's not so bad—but that's exactly what credit card companies want you to think.

Let's look at some real figures to see how bad it really is. So if your balance is $100, you actually owe them $121. Also keep in mind that interest is charged on unpaid balances. Now here comes the trick. When you receive your next statement and your minimum payment is $10, that is not enough to cover your interest of $21. The only way to get your balance back to $0.00 is to have some money going toward the principle. Your next statement will be more than the last because you paid nothing toward the principal or unpaid balance. If you continually pay the minimum, you will never pay your bill off because it will continuously increase. Remember, when the first payment was made, you were paying 21% or $21 on $100; and because you paid only $10 of the $21 owed for interest, your next payment will be $111 at 21% interest. You do the math. The figures I just used were not realistic but used as an example to show you how interest and minimum payments work.

The average balance on credit cards in this country is anywhere from $10,000 to $15,000. Let's do the math on these real numbers and we will see just how much financial trouble so many people are in. We'll just use the $10,000 debt at 21% which computes to a total of $2100. This will continually climb if only the minimum payment is paid. Scary, right? So many people have unknowingly fallen into this trap that the government has now stepped in, forcing credit card companies to raise the minimum payment. I am not sure, but I believe it has to be enough to cover the interest. In this illustration, I used the 21% interest rate. Your actual interest rate may be lower, but the principle is the same. Just multiply your interest rate by your balance and you will see what your actual balance will be. You have to find a way to pay toward your principle! That's the only way to get out of debt!

CHAPTER 6
What Type of Insurance?
Who to Cover?
How Much to Get?

Before I try to answer any of the questions in the title of this chapter, let me go on record as saying that it is not my purpose or my right to tell you what to buy or not to buy, but to help you become an informed buyer. The choices are strictly up to you. In my lifetime, I have gained quite a bit of knowledge of how insurance works. When purchasing insurance, do not be afraid to ask the tough questions. Ask your agent to explain all the perks they will tell you about and how they work. Remember, insurance agents are salesmen who have been well-schooled in highlighting the positive while downplaying the negatives.

First of all, let's deal with the two primary types of life insurance. The first one, and the one you will probably hear about the most, is "whole life." It is called that because you will be paying for it your whole life. You should ask if the policy is one that can be paid up. One of their strongest selling points is that whole life policies have cash value from which you can borrow.

They also have a savings plan where they save money for you in the policy. You should ask your agent when you can borrow money, how much you can borrow, how that will affect your face value, and where the money that they are saving comes from. Ask if they overcharge you for your policy and if the excess is what they are saving for you— using your money for their savings. Ask them if you have to repay borrowed money and does the amount borrowed accrue interest. Let's say that you get a $50,000 whole life policy and you borrow $10,000; your face value is now $40,000 and you have to pay them back the $10,000 with interest. Your face value will go back up as you repay. This is okay as long as you understand that, if something should happen to the policy holder, the beneficiary would receive only $40,000 plus the amount that has been repaid. The primary question would be, "Why do I have to pay back *my* money with interest?"

Another thing you should know is that the money they take out of your payment or saving goes into an interest-making account for them. The insurance company will make tons of interest for years off your money, but you will never see a dime of it. Let's assume that you never borrow from your $50,000 policy and you live 50 years and die. All your beneficiary will receive is $50,000. What happens to all of that interest they made off your money that they had been saving for you? What happened to *your* savings? Ask your agent these questions.

The second kind of life insurance is called term life. It is just what it says—it's only for a term. This is the kind that most businesses provide for their employees. We are not talking about health insurance; we are talking about life insurance. Most term policies are for a term of 20 years, based on your age. The major selling point is that it is so much cheaper. There is no cash value, meaning that there is no savings and you cannot borrow from it. It will work only for the very disciplined person and I'll explain why.

Remember, the sole purpose for insurance is to replace lost income. There is an upside and a downside and I'll explain both. Here is how the upside works. You can buy term life insurance much cheaper than whole life. Let's use the same amount for term as we did for whole life insurance: $50,000. The numbers I am about to use are only for an example to make it easy to understand. You buy term insurance for about half of the cost of whole life. For example: A person bought a $50,000 whole life policy and was paying $600 per month; but he could get the same $50,000 term insurance for about $300 per month. Keep in mind that term will only last 20 years. This is why it is good only for the very disciplined person. You have been paying $600 faithfully, but now you've got the same amount and the same coverage for $300, but how can this work in your favor? For 20 years, take the $300 that you are saving and put it faithfully into of an interest-bearing savings vehicle. After 20 years, even with interest, you would have saved $72,000!

Now let's look at the downside. Remember, your coverage was only for 20 years, and those years have ended. Now you have to make a decision. But before you do, let's look at your financial status. You have saved $72,000 plus about $10,000 interest, which totals $82,000—plus your 401K. Now you can choose to renew your policy, which will cost a little more because you are 20 years older; or you can say, "I am close to retirement age with well over $100,000 plus my retirement check, and the kids are all gone; so do I really need more insurance?" Remember, that insurance is only to cover lost income—and you haven't lost any.

Now let's look at who should be covered. When it comes to insurance and who should be covered, we must determine what type of insurance we are talking about. For health insurance, everyone in the home should be covered; but when it comes to life insurance, there are some decisions that have to be made. Again, we must remember the purpose of life insurance—to replace lost income so that loved ones can carry on. So the question is—should young children be insured? It's a gamble, but maybe not one worth taking; because in most cases, the children will live to be adults. But if you feel better about doing so, go right ahead because to insure a young healthy child is very inexpensive.

Now we need to know how much coverage is needed. All of this must be based on what the survivor's needs will be in order to maintain the same lifestyle for a given period. Remember, the purpose of insurance is to replace lost income, not to make the survivor rich. Of course, if that's what a person wants to do, that's okay. In case of the husband's death, he would want his family to be taken care of for whatever period of time that they agree on. But all of this is totally up to those who are involved and should be mutually agreed upon. Most of the time, the husband is the most highly insured; but that too is a family decision.

Another important thing to be aware of is that age is a huge factor. A young healthy man with no bad habits can get a lot more insurance and at a lot cheaper cost than an older man, even if the older man is still in good health. The insurance company is gambling on you living a very long time. That's how they profit. The longer they don't have to pay out any money, the longer they gain interest on your premium.

CHAPTER 7
How to Get Out of Debt

This is an age old question that has been asked down through the corridors of time, but the answer still eludes many. For this reason, some of you will never get out of debt—not because you didn't know how, but because you were not willing to put forth the necessary effort to do so. There is nothing magical about this book, though it can work like magic if you will embrace its principles and put them into practice. Too many seem to think they can just "wish" themselves out of debt without putting any work into it. Even faith without works is dead.

There was an elderly lady who attended the same church that my wife attended in her teens. My wife said that, on several pages of the lady's Bible and next to many scriptures, you would see the letters "T" and "P." One day, my wife asked the lady what those letters meant and why they were located only next to certain scriptures. Her reply

39

was, "Every scripture that you find letters next to, I have 'TRIED' and 'PROVED' them." That is much the same that you will find in my following statements, because everything that I will write about is from my personal experiences; and, like the old lady, I can say, "I have tried and proved them!"

My wife and I have been completely out of debt twice during our marriage and would have still been out had it not been for a business deal that went south because we failed to do our homework. We are on our way out again by using the same methods that got us out before. I will be sharing these methods with you in this chapter.

We have accomplished a lot of things working together for these 45 years. We have reached many goals, including financial ones. We have paid over $40,000 toward our mortgage in just two years using the very same method that I will share with you. We have paid off six houses, and one of them we have paid off twice. As I told you before, I am writing from experience, and we are just ordinary people with ordinary jobs.

I worked for Ford Motor Company and my wife worked for the U.S. government. If we can do it, so can you if you follow the methods detailed in this book. Let's share these methods. The figures I will be using will be examples and may or may not fit your situation.

You begin by using some plain envelopes. The number of envelopes you will need will be determined by the number of bills you want to pay off. Include only those things that can be paid off—credit cards, vehicles, loans, etc. Don't even include your mortgage in this section; I will deal with it alone. We'll use five envelopes to show you how it works.

On the first envelope you will write the name and the pay-off amount of the smallest bill; on the second, the next smallest amount; and so on to the fifth, which will be the largest bill. For example, let's say your smallest bill is $1000, then the next one $2000, $3000, $4000, and the fifth is $5000. These will be the numbers on each envelope. The key is to get the first one paid off and the others will work like magic.

Let's say that your payment on the first one is $100, second is $200, third, $300, fourth, $400 and the fifth is $500. The fastest way to pay any bill off is by paying extra on the principle or unpaid balance. Where will this extra money come from? There are two places. The first is discretionary money. This is money that is left over after all of your bills are paid—what we call extra money. If this is your case, then it will be a great way to start paying off that first bill.

But what if there is no discretionary income? The second way is the most difficult; and it will only work based on how badly you want to get out of debt, because it will call for some sacrificing. You will have to give up something for a period of time. This will not be a long time, but it can be done and it's necessary if you are serious about getting out of debt. You won't have to cut back on the whole, but just a portion. Here are a few suggestions. Instead of going to the movie every week, go every two weeks; instead of eating in the cafeteria at work every day, begin taking a lunch; go to restaurants on the weekend instead of every day of the week; cut back on your recreation until that first bill is paid off; start making your children a school lunch—they do not have to eat in the school's cafeteria every day. Now, take the saved money that you sacrificed and put it toward that first bill. It really won't take as long as you might think, and the results will be rewarding. Once you have gotten that first bill paid off, the magical part comes in. Oh, let me stop here before I forget and remind you that while you are paying the first bill, you must continue paying the other four as usual.

Okay, now that you have paid off the first bill, you have some discretionary income--$100. Take $100 and put with the $200 that you have been paying on the second bill. Now you'll be paying $300 per month on the second bill. You will find that it won't take long to pay off bill number two either. When you pay off number two, take $100 from number one, plus the $200 from number two and put it to the $300 that you are paying on bill number three. Now you are doubling up on number three with $600. Do the same with four and five. Soon you will be out of debt except for your mortgage. But by paying off those five debts, you have created quite a bit of discretionary income—to the tune of $1500! You are now in great shape to pay off your mortgage.

Now here is the formula for paying off your mortgage. This will be based on the status of your credit. You will need to get a line of credit in the amount of $10,000, but you want it to be an INTEREST ONLY account, which means that your payments will be for interest; and this won't be very much because you will be paying interest only on what you use. You will not be paying on $10,000, but only on the amount you use. The $1500 discretionary money will be far more than the interest charge because interest is calculated monthly. You'll understand it better when you see the program that you will be using.

The program works like this. You have $10,000 that you can borrow from. Let's say that you bought a $200,000 house and your monthly payment is $1200. If your interest rate is 5%, only about $35 of the $1200 pay will go toward the principal. The way mortgage companies work is about 95%

of your payments will go toward interest. The payment on our home was $1135; at the end of the year when we got our statement, we had paid only $335 toward the principle! All the rest of over $12,000 went toward interest. Through this program, you must keep in the forefront of your mind that interest is paid on the unpaid balance. Your total focus must be to decrease the unpaid balance as quickly as possible so all of your discretionary income goes toward the unpaid balance or principle.

Now back to the program. You will borrow $3000 from your line of credit to send it, along with your regular monthly payment, to the mortgage company along with a note instructing them to apply the $3000 to your principle. You will also ask them to send a confirmation that it was applied as you requested. In one payment, you have knocked your principle down by $3000. Now they will charge you interest on a principle that has been reduced by $3000, which is a big difference. This means that your next month's payment will have more going toward your principle. How will we pay back the $3000? Do you remember the $1500 discretionary income? Send it to whoever your line of credit is with, and in the two months, you will have repaid the $3000 that you borrowed from your line of credit. At that point, borrow another $3000 and apply it toward your principle, and in four months you will have reduced your principle by $6000, which again is very huge. Pay this $3000 just as you did the others. At this pace, by paying your principle down by $3000 every two months, at the end of one year, you would have paid your principle down by $18,000! THAT'S HUGE!!! Now your $200,000 principle that you began with is down to $182,000. It will actually be less than that because each $3000 paid against your principle caused more of your monthly payment to go toward your principle. So this trend will be continual down through the years until eventually all of your monthly payments will be applied to your principle.

Based on the figures we used above, you would have wiped out a 30-year mortgage in just 11 years, saving yourself about $200,000 in interest. Congratulations!! I know this to be true, because if you take 30 years to pay off your house, you will pay three times more than its selling price.

CHAPTER 8
How to Stay Out of Debt

Again, this is an age old question and the sad truth and answer is that most people don't stay out of debt because they fall into that "now I can" deadly trap. "Now I can buy this and that"—and before they realize what hit them, they are right back into what they worked so hard to get out of. You really have to be careful and disciplined because now that you are out of debt, that discretionary money has skyrocketed. Debt is like trouble—it's a lot easier to get into that it is to get out of.

I'm going to say something here that I intended to say earlier—Anytime you pay off a bill, treat it as if you hadn't. For example: Your car payment is $400 per month. When you pay it off and it still runs good, treat it as if you still have the payment. It is very important to keep it due on the same date of the month; and when that date comes, write a check for the exact amount. But instead of putting the bank's name on it, put your name on it. We know that somewhere down the road you will need to buy another car, the money you have saved can be used for a nice down payment. Maybe you have enough to pay cash, but if you can't, you should have quite a bit of discretionary money. Just be wise and know where the money for the new car will come from. In other words, sit down and count the cost. A very wise man asked the question, "What man is it that when he decides to build a house doesn't sit down first to see if he has everything that he needs to build it?" Remember, if a man doesn't learn from his first mistake, he will make a second one. Everyone is not disciplined enough to own a credit card. Credit cards are among the top reasons that so many people are drowning in debt. You have to be honest with yourself. If you know that you cannot control your spending, then this is a sign that you do not need a credit card. It's okay to have some debt as long as it's manageable.

CHAPTER 9
Is It Okay to Buy on Credit?

If you are one of those who does not pay his bills on time—
or does not pay them at all, the answer is a definite, "NO! It
is NOT okay for you to buy on credit!" If you are disciplined
and understand the concept of principle and interest, sit
down before you buy to see if you have the wherewithal to
repay the loan; then it's okay to buy on credit.

There are two concepts among financial planners. One will
encourage you to buy on credit even if you have the money
up front. Their philosophy is "Why use your money (which
could stay in the bank and make interest) when you can use
their money?" The other philosophy is just the opposite.
They will say, "Why buy on credit and pay interest when you
have enough money to pay for it up front?" There is no right
or wrong here; it is just a matter of choice and personality.
Both will work; you have to choose which best fits your
outlook. I have used both concepts with great success.

51

As I mentioned earlier, my wife has a credit card that pays her to use it, so there are times when we will use it for the financial benefits. Many times when we go on vacation, we use this card to pay for rental car, hotels, and some other things related to vacation. It also makes for keeping good records. As soon as we get back home, we figure out the total amount we spent and pay the bill in full when it arrives. The downside of the second philosophy is that if you are not careful and disciplined, when you return home with pocket full of cash, you could be tempted to spend it.

We bought all our furniture on credit and also our carpet. There are some legitimate businesses that will allow you to buy their product and give you one to two years to pay. You must still do your homework and understand the whole contract though, because it can be tricky. You could end up in a financial mess. Here are some things that you should know. Their contract will read: *Buy with no down payment and no interest for one or two years.* This one is very tricky because they have left something out. The words they left out are "no payment." I got caught in this one once. The three things you want to hear is "no down payment," "no payments," and "no interest." Here is how this thing works. It's much like when you buy a car; you have to be approved by some lending institution. Once you are approved, the lender pays the dealership in full and your payment is made to the lender. This is the exact same method that these businesses use; the moment they sell you their product, you have to be approved by some lending institution that pays them in full. You then pay that institution. The bad part about it is that the lending institution is usually a high interest loan company whose interest rate is around 21%, which is dangerously high. It is true that you have the two or three years to pay, but at the end of two years, if you have not paid the full payment or if you are one day late, they are going to retroact (change) your interest for the whole two years. This is what they are gambling will happen—that you will not be able to pay in full. It can be a great way to purchase, but only if you use your head. We have done it many times, but you have to beat them at their own game.

"How do I beat them at their own game?" you might ask. If you are dealing with the one year program, take the total amount owed and divide it by twelve; and whatever that number comes out to be, you must put that amount away for twelve months. Example: If your purchase totals $2400, divide that number by twelve and you will come up with $200. That is the amount you need to save every month; and if you do so, you will have the $2400 needed to pay off the debt. I usually go in about two days before the deadline and pay the debt in full. I have done this so many times— and each and every time, they try to talk me out of it. Why? They are going to lose a lot of money in interest on me because I paid only the purchase price. Unfortunately, they will make up for this on those ninety-nine other people who will not pay it off in the time provided.

Companies are constantly coming up with gimmicks, like "buy one, get one free" to make you think you are getting a deal. There is no such thing, and if that were true they would go out of business. Always be aware of the large letters in an advertisement, because in most cases this is not where the truth lies. If you want to see the real truth, read the fine print. Someone said, "The big letters give, but the little letters take away." Other familiar quotes say, "If it sounds too good to be true, it probably is"—and "anything too sweet will sour." It's okay to buy on credit—if you "buy smart!"

CONCLUSION

In conclusion, I want to thank all who have bought this book, and I hope that you have enjoyed reading it as much as I enjoyed writing it. I also hope that it has changed some bad financial habits into some good ones. One of the main goals of this book was to show how easy it is to save and to understand the importance of discipline. I hope you have turned from an "I wish and hope I can" outlook to "I believe I can and know I can and I will" outlook. If you will apply the things you have read in this book, all of the above is certainly possible and will come to pass. You have to see yourself accomplishing these things. If I did it, you can do it. Get away from that mentality of your momma, your teacher or anyone else who told you that you would never become anything. Prove them wrong!!!

ABOUT THE AUTHOR

Rev. Wade P. Hooks Sr. is a licensed and ordained minister, with a master's degree in theology from the Southern California School of Ministry. He accepted the Lord in 1962, shortly after moving to Michigan from Alabama.

Rev. Hooks places great value on integrity, transparency, and honesty. He is a hard worker who loves and provides for his family. He accepted his call to ministry in 1972, and has worked faithfully in his calling since that time. Prior to accepting his call to the ministry, he worked in various capacities within the church—usher, trustee, teacher and youth leader. Rev. Hooks has a very unique gift of "story telling" which he often uses in his sermons. Drawing from his personal life experiences, he makes the Scriptures come alive, often with a bit of humor, thus bringing understanding of the Word to where we live today. Rev. Hooks is truly an inspiration to many.

www.ingramcontent.com/pod-product-compliance
Lightning Source LLC
Chambersburg PA
CBHW060721030426

42337CB00017B/2947